My Father's Story

A Prompted Journal for Sharing Memories

© **Copyright 2024 by Abbix Publishing Company - All rights reserved.**

The content contained within this book may not be reproduced, duplicated, or transmitted without direct written permission from the author or the publisher.

Under no circumstances will any blame or legal responsibility be held against the publisher, or author, for any damages, reparation, or monetary loss due to the information contained within this book, either directly or indirectly.

Legal Notice:

This book is copyright protected. It is only for personal use. You cannot amend, distribute, sell, use, quote or paraphrase any part, or the content within this book, without the consent of the author or publisher.

Disclaimer Notice:

Please note the information contained within this document is for educational and entertainment purposes only. All effort has been executed to present accurate, up-to-date, reliable, complete information. No warranties of any kind are declared or implied. Readers acknowledge that the author is not engaging in the rendering of legal, financial, medical, or professional advice. The content within this book has been derived from various sources. Please consult a licensed professional before attempting any techniques outlined in this book.

By reading this document, the reader agrees that under no circumstances is the author responsible for any losses, direct or indirect, that are incurred as a result of the use of information contained within this document, including, but not limited to, errors, omissions, or inaccuracies.

Contents

1. Introduction — 5
2. Early Years — 9
3. Family Heritage — 18
4. School Days — 27
5. Friends and Adventures — 36
6. Teenage Years — 45
7. Love and Relationships — 54
8. College and Early Adulthood — 63
9. Career Journey — 72
10. Marriage and Parenthood — 81
11. Hobbies and Interests — 90
12. Life Lessons and Values — 96
13. Challenges and Triumphs — 105
14. Reflections and Future Hopes — 114
15. Letters to the Ones that I Love — 123

Introduction

A father's love is the foundation of a strong family.
– Author Unknown

What inspired you to start this journal?

....
....
....
....
....
....
....
....
....
....

What do you hope to achieve by documenting your life story?

....
....
....
....
....
....
....
....
....
....

How do you feel about sharing your personal experiences and memories?

....
....
....
....
....
....
....
....
....
....
....

What specific topics or events are you most excited to write about?

....
....
....
....
....
....
....
....
....
....
....

What are your goals for this journaling journey?

Early Years

*Childhood is where dreams are woven
into the fabric of our being.*

– Author Unknown

Place a Picture Here

What is your birthdate and place of birth?

....
....
....
....
....
....
....
....
....
....

Describe your childhood home.

....
....
....
....
....
....
....
....
....
....

What were your parents like? What did they do for a living?

....
....
....
....
....
....
....
....
....
....

Do you have any siblings? What are your favorite memories with them?

....
....
....
....
....
....
....
....
....
....

What were some of your favorite childhood games or activities?

....
....
....
....
....
....
....
....
....
....

Who were your best friends growing up?

....
....
....
....
....
....
....
....
....
....

Did you have any pets? Tell a story about one.

....
....
....
....
....
....
....
....
....
....

What were some of your family traditions?

....
....
....
....
....
....
....
....
....
....

Describe a memorable family vacation or trip.

....
....
....
....
....
....
....
....
....
....

What was the most valuable lesson you learned from your parents?

....
....
....
....
....
....
....
....
....
....

What values were important to your family?

....
....
....
....
....
....
....
....
....
....

Describe a typical family meal.

....
....
....
....
....
....
....
....
....
....
....

Did you have any chores or responsibilities as a child?

....
....
....
....
....
....
....
....
....

What was your favorite holiday and why?

....
....
....
....
....
....
....
....
....
....

What are your earliest childhood memories?

Family Heritage

The roots of a family tree begin with the love of a father.
– Author Unknown

Place a Picture Here

What do you know about your family's ancestry?

....
....
....
....
....
....
....
....
....
....

Where did your ancestors come from?

....
....
....
....
....
....
....
....
....
....

Have you ever visited the places your ancestors came from?

....
....
....
....
....
....
....
....
....
....

What family traditions have been passed down through generations?

....
....
....
....
....
....
....
....
....
....

Are there any family heirlooms or keepsakes with special significance?

....
....
....
....
....
....
....
....
....
....

What languages were spoken in your family?

....
....
....
....
....
....
....
....
....
....

Did your family celebrate any unique holidays or festivals?

....
....
....
....
....
....
....
....
....
....

What stories did your grandparents tell you?

....
....
....
....
....
....
....
....
....
....

What are some cultural practices that were important to your family?

....
....
....
....
....
....
....
....
....
....

How has your family heritage influenced your identity?

....
....
....
....
....
....
....
....
....
....

Are there any famous or notable people in your family history?

....
....
....
....
....
....
....
....
....

What was your relationship like with your grandparents?

....
....
....
....
....
....
....
....
....
....

Did your family have any special recipes or foods?

....
....
....
....
....
....
....
....
....
....

How did your family come to live in the place you grew up?

....
....
....
....
....
....
....
....
....
....

What family stories have you passed down to your children?

School Days

Education opens doors to endless possibilities.
– Author Unknown

What was the name of your elementary school?

....
....
....
....
....
....
....
....
....
....

What was your favorite subject in school?

....
....
....
....
....
....
....
....
....
....

Who was your favorite teacher and why?

....
....
....
....
....
....
....
....
....
....

Describe your most memorable first day of school.

....
....
....
....
....
....
....
....
....
....

Did you enjoy school? Why or why not?

....
....
....
....
....
....
....
....
....
....

What extracurricular activities did you participate in?

....
....
....
....
....
....
....
....
....

Did you have a favorite book or story as a child?

....
....
....
....
....
....
....
....
....
....
....

What were recess and lunchtime like?

....
....
....
....
....
....
....
....
....
....
....

Did you ever get into trouble at school? What happened?

....
....
....
....
....
....
....
....
....
....

What achievements or awards did you earn in school?

....
....
....
....
....
....
....
....
....
....

How did you get to and from school?

....
....
....
....
....
....
....
....
....
....

Describe a typical school day.

....
....
....
....
....
....
....
....
....
....

What was your least favorite subject and why?

....
....
....
....
....
....
....
....
....

What did you want to be when you grew up?

....
....
....
....
....
....
....
....
....

What advice would you give to your school-age self?

Friends and Adventures

*Adventure awaits those who seek it
with friends by their side.*

– Author Unknown

Place a Picture Here

Who was your best friend growing up?

....
....
....
....
....
....
....
....
....
....

What adventures did you and your friends go on?

....
....
....
....
....
....
....
....
....
....
....

Describe a memorable sleepover or playdate.

....
....
....
....
....
....
....
....
....
....

Did you and your friends have any secret clubs or groups?

....
....
....
....
....
....
....
....
....
....

What games did you play with your friends?

....
....
....
....
....
....
....
....
....

What was your favorite place to hang out with friends?

....
....
....
....
....
....
....
....
....
....

Did you and your friends have any nicknames for each other?

....
....
....
....
....
....
....
....
....
....

Did you have any pen pals or long-distance friends?

....
....
....
....
....
....
....
....
....
....

What was a typical weekend like with your friends?

Did you and your friends have any special traditions or rituals?

Describe a funny or embarrassing moment with your friends.

....
....
....
....
....
....
....
....
....
....

What was the best gift you ever received from a friend?

....
....
....
....
....
....
....
....
....
....

Did you ever have a falling out with a friend? How did you resolve it?

....
....
....
....
....
....
....
....
....
....

Who were your childhood role models or heroes?

....
....
....
....
....
....
....
....
....
....

How have your friendships shaped who you are today?

Teenage Years

*The teenage years are a journey of
self-discovery and growth.*

– Author Unknown

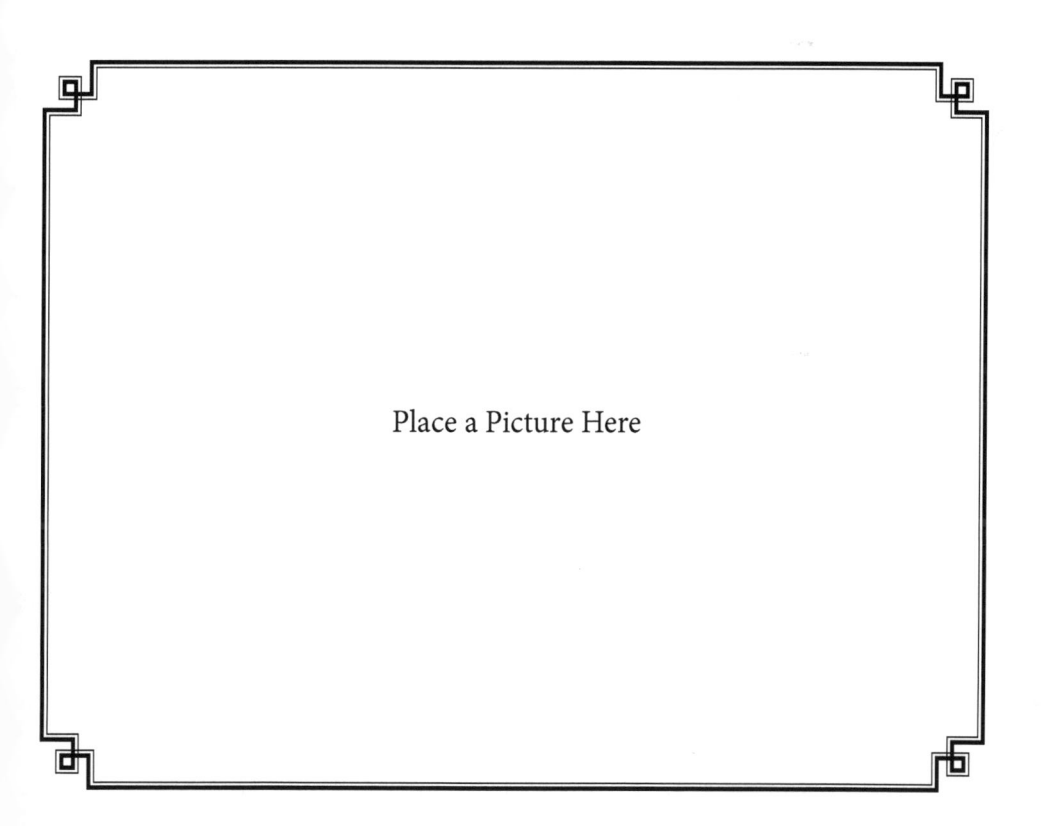

Place a Picture Here

What was your teenage bedroom like?

....
....
....
....
....
....
....
....
....
....

How did you spend your free time as a teenager?

....
....
....
....
....
....
....
....
....
....

What music did you listen to during your teenage years?

....
....
....
....
....
....
....
....
....
....

Describe your first job.

....
....
....
....
....
....
....
....
....
....

What were your teenage hobbies and interests?

....
....
....
....
....
....
....
....
....
....

How did you balance school and social life?

....
....
....
....
....
....
....
....
....
....

What was your most memorable high school experience?

....
....
....
....
....
....
....
....
....
....

Did you play any sports in high school?

....
....
....
....
....
....
....
....
....
....

What was your favorite high school class?

....
....
....
....
....
....
....
....
....
....

Did you attend your high school prom? What was it like?

....
....
....
....
....
....
....
....
....
....

What was your favorite fashion trend as a teenager?

....
....
....
....
....
....
....
....
....
....

Who was your first crush or significant other?

....
....
....
....
....
....
....
....
....
....

How did you spend your summer vacations as a teenager?

....
....
....
....
....
....
....
....
....
....

Did you have a favorite hangout spot?

....
....
....
....
....
....
....
....
....
....

What advice would you give to your teenage self?

Love and Relationships

Love is the thread that weaves our lives together.
– Author Unknown

Place a Picture Here

Who was your first love?

....
....
....
....
....
....
....
....
....
....

How did you meet your significant other?

....
....
....
....
....
....
....
....
....
....

Describe your first date.

....
....
....
....
....
....
....
....
....
....

When did you know you were in love?

....
....
....
....
....
....
....
....
....
....

How did you and your partner decide to get engaged?

....
....
....
....
....
....
....
....
....
....

What are your favorite memories with your partner?

....
....
....
....
....
....
....
....
....
....

How do you handle disagreements in your relationship?

....
....
....
....
....
....
....
....
....

What do you appreciate most about your partner?

....
....
....
....
....
....
....
....
....
....

What advice would you give to someone looking for love?

....
....
....
....
....
....
....
....
....
....

How do you keep the romance alive in your relationship?

....
....
....
....
....
....
....
....
....
....

What qualities do you value most in a partner?

....
....
....
....
....
....
....
....
....
....

Describe a challenging time in your relationship and how you overcame it.

....
....
....
....
....
....
....
....
....
....

How has your relationship changed over the years?

....
....
....
....
....
....
....
....
....
....

What is your favorite thing to do together as a couple?

....
....
....
....
....
....
....
....
....
....

How do you support each other's dreams and goals?

College and Early Adulthood

The future is built on the dreams of today.
— Author Unknown

Place a Picture Here

Where did you go to college?

....
....
....
....
....
....
....
....
....
....

What was your major and why did you choose it?

....
....
....
....
....
....
....
....
....
....

Describe your college campus.

....
....
....
....
....
....
....
....
....
....

What was your first day of college like?

....
....
....
....
....
....
....
....
....
....

Did you live on campus or commute?

Who were your college roommates?

What clubs or organizations did you join in college?

....
....
....
....
....
....
....
....
....
....

What was your favorite college class?

....
....
....
....
....
....
....
....
....
....

How did you manage your time between classes and social life?

....
....
....
....
....
....
....
....
....
....

Describe a memorable college party or event.

....
....
....
....
....
....
....
....
....
....

What internships or work experiences did you have during college?

....
....
....
....
....
....
....
....
....
....

Who were your college friends and how did you meet them?

....
....
....
....
....
....
....
....
....
....

What advice would you give to current college students?

....
....
....
....
....
....
....
....
....
....

What was your graduation day like?

....
....
....
....
....
....
....
....
....
....

What were your career aspirations after college?

Career Journey

Passion in your work brings purpose to your life.
– Author Unknown

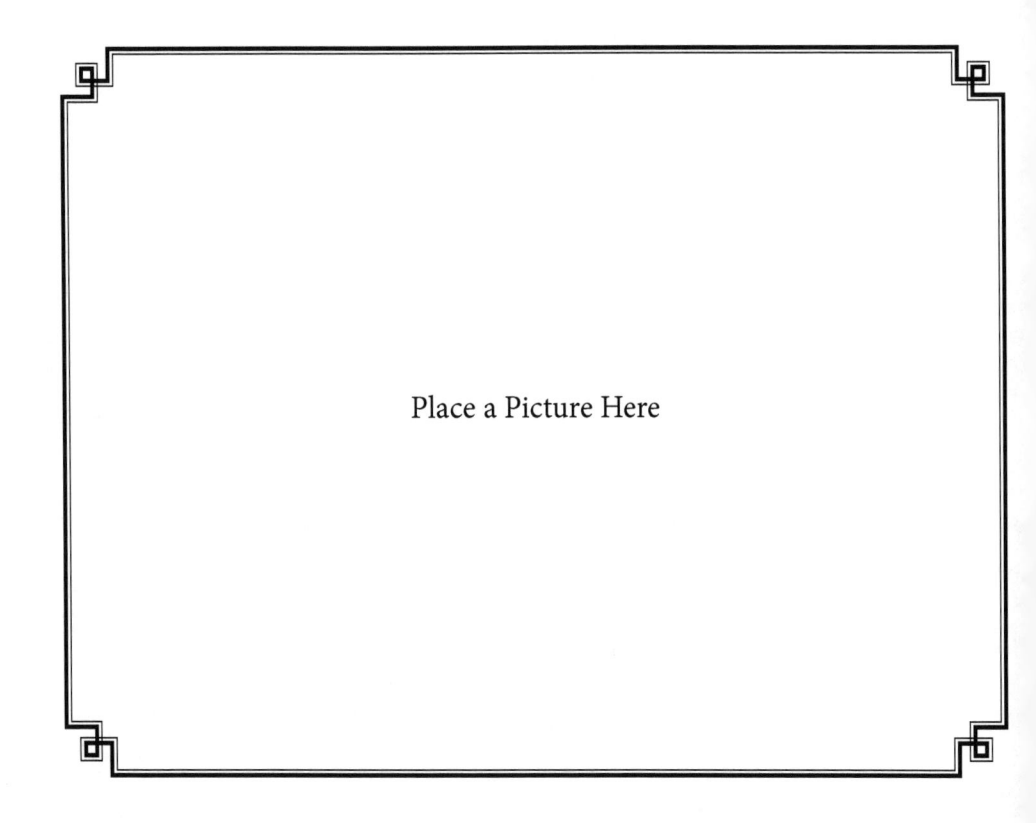

Place a Picture Here

What was your first job?

....
....
....
....
....
....
....
....
....
....

What motivated you to choose your career path?

....
....
....
....
....
....
....
....
....
....

Describe your typical workday.

....
....
....
....
....
....
....
....
....
....

Who were your mentors or role models in your career?

....
....
....
....
....
....
....
....
....
....

What were the biggest challenges you faced in your career?

....
....
....
....
....
....
....
....
....
....

What accomplishments are you most proud of?

....
....
....
....
....
....
....
....
....
....

How did you balance work and personal life?

....
....
....
....
....
....
....
....
....
....

What skills did you develop throughout your career?

....
....
....
....
....
....
....
....
....
....

Describe a memorable project or achievement at work.

....
....
....
....
....
....
....
....
....
....
....

How did you handle career setbacks or failures?

....
....
....
....
....
....
....
....
....
....
....
....

What was your favorite job and why?

....
....
....
....
....
....
....
....
....
....

Who were your favorite colleagues or coworkers?

....
....
....
....
....
....
....
....
....
....

What was the most rewarding aspect of your career?

Did you ever switch careers? If so, why and how did you manage the transition?

What legacy do you hope to leave through your work?

Marriage and Parenthood

A father's heart is the anchor that keeps the family steady.
– Author Unknown

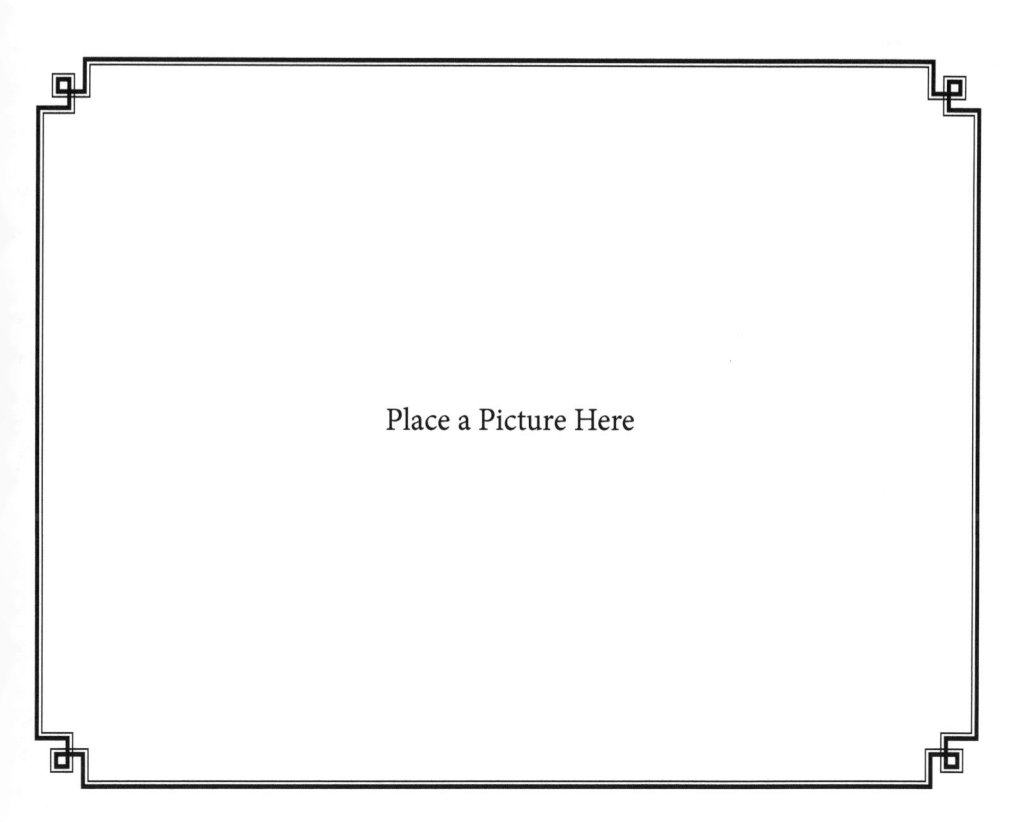

Place a Picture Here

How long were you and your partner engaged before you got married?

....
....
....
....
....
....
....
....
....
....

What was your wedding day like?

....
....
....
....
....
....
....
....
....
....

Describe the early years of your marriage.

....
....
....
....
....
....
....
....
....
....

When did you decide to start a family?

....
....
....
....
....
....
....
....
....
....

How did you feel when you found out you were going to be a parent?

Describe the day your first child was born.

How did you choose your child/children's names?

....
....
....
....
....
....
....
....
....
....

What was the most surprising thing about becoming a parent?

....
....
....
....
....
....
....
....
....
....
....

What are your favorite memories of your child/children's early years?

....
....
....
....
....
....
....
....
....
....

How did you handle the challenges of parenting?

....
....
....
....
....
....
....
....
....
....

What family traditions did you create?

How did you support your child/children's interests and hobbies?

Describe a memorable family vacation.

....
....
....
....
....
....
....
....
....
....

What is the most important lesson you've learned from being a parent?

....
....
....
....
....
....
....
....
....
....

How do you hope your child/children remember their childhood?

Hobbies and Interests

Hobbies are the spice that add flavor to our lives.
— Author Unknown

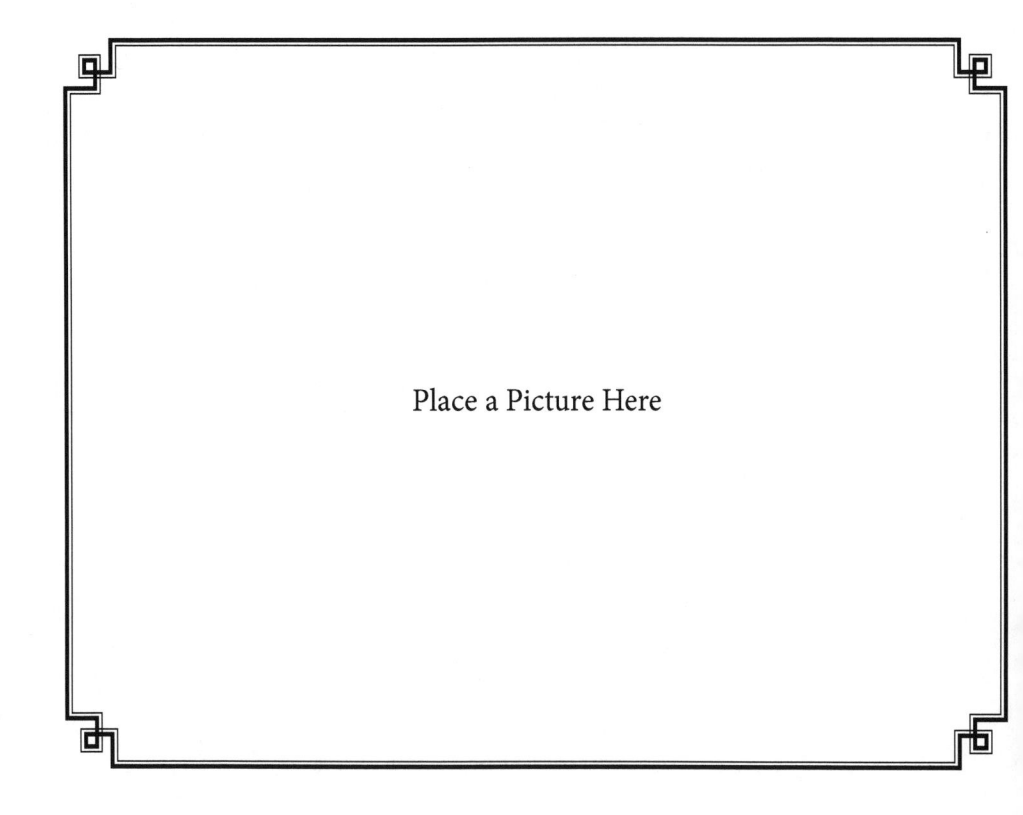

Place a Picture Here

What are your favorite hobbies and interests?

....
....
....
....
....
....
....
....
....
....

How did you discover your passion for your hobbies?

....
....
....
....
....
....
....
....
....
....

What role do hobbies play in your life?

....
....
....
....
....
....
....
....
....
....

What is the most unusual or unique hobby you have?

....
....
....
....
....
....
....
....
....
....

How do your hobbies help you relax and unwind?

....
....
....
....
....
....
....
....
....
....

What is your favorite memory related to your hobbies?

....
....
....
....
....
....
....
....
....
....

How have your hobbies evolved over time?

....
....
....
....
....
....
....
....
....

How do your hobbies reflect your personality and interests?

....
....
....
....
....
....
....
....
....

What advice would you give to someone looking to discover new hobbies?

....
....
....
....
....
....
....
....
....
....

What new hobbies or interests would you like to explore?

....
....
....
....
....
....
....
....
....
....

Life Lessons and Values

*Life's lessons are the seeds of wisdom
we plant along the way.*

– Author Unknown

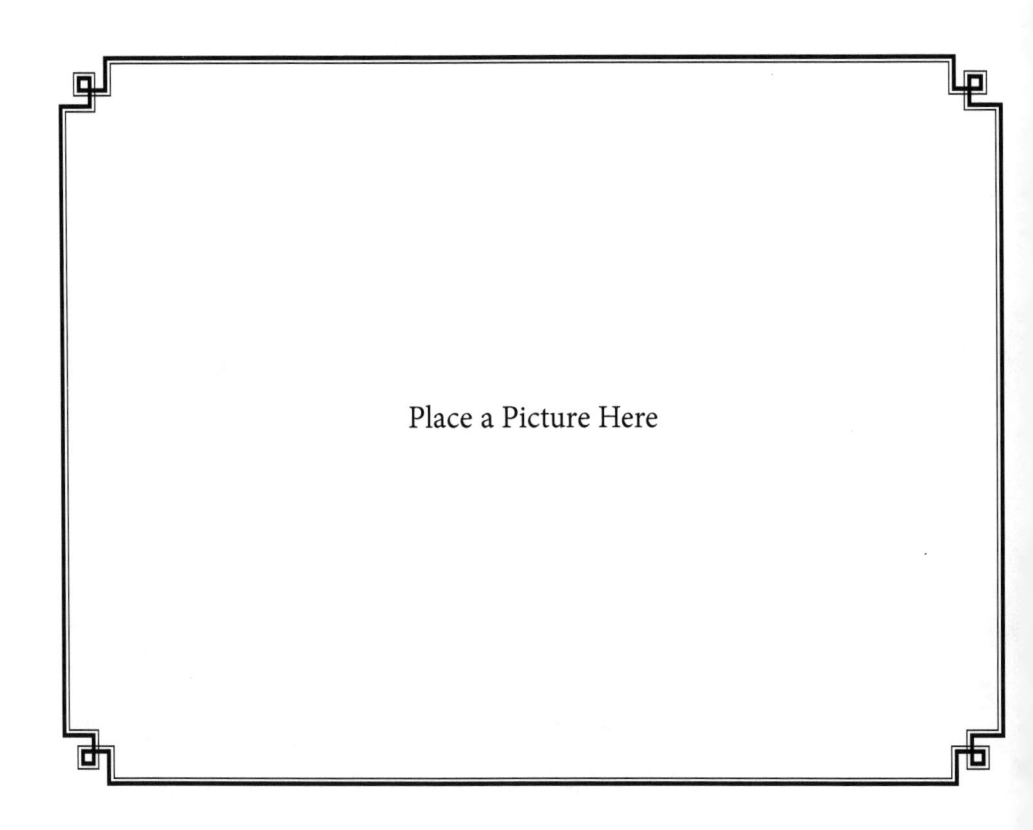

Place a Picture Here

What are the most important values you live by?

....
....
....
....
....
....
....
....
....
....

Who taught you these values?

....
....
....
....
....
....
....
....
....
....

What life experiences shaped your values?

....
....
....
....
....
....
....
....
....
....

How do you pass on your values to others?

....
....
....
....
....
....
....
....
....
....

What is the most important lesson you've learned in life?

....
....
....
....
....
....
....
....
....
....

How do you handle difficult situations?

....
....
....
....
....
....
....
....
....
....

What role does integrity play in your life?

....
....
....
....
....
....
....
....
....
....

How do you define success?

....
....
....
....
....
....
....
....
....
....

What are your views on failure and how to overcome it?

....
....
....
....
....
....
....
....
....
....

How do you handle stress and adversity?

....
....
....
....
....
....
....
....
....
....
....

What role does gratitude play in your life?

....
....
....
....
....
....
....
....
....
....

How do you practice kindness and compassion?

....
....
....
....
....
....
....
....
....
....

What values do you hope to instill in your child/children?

....
....
....
....
....
....
....
....
....
....

What are your views on forgiveness and letting go?

....
....
....
....
....
....
....
....
....
....

What is the best piece of advice you've ever received?

Challenges and Triumphs

Overcoming challenges is the pathway to triumph.
– Author Unknown

Place a Picture Here

What was the biggest challenge you faced in your life?

....
....
....
....
....
....
....
....
....

How do you find strength in difficult times?

....
....
....
....
....
....
....
....
....

Describe a time when you felt truly accomplished.

....
....
....
....
....
....
....
....
....
....

What are you most proud of in your life?

....
....
....
....
....
....
....
....
....
....

How do you handle setbacks and failures?

....
....
....
....
....
....
....
....
....
....

What are your strategies for managing stress?

....
....
....
....
....
....
....
....
....
....

What motivates you to keep going during tough times?

....
....
....
....
....
....
....
....
....
....

Describe a time when you had to make a difficult decision.

....
....
....
....
....
....
....
....
....
....

How do you stay positive in the face of adversity?

....
....
....
....
....
....
....
....
....
....

What support systems do you rely on during challenging times?

....
....
....
....
....
....
....
....
....
....

What role does self-belief play in your life?

....
....
....
....
....
....
....
....
....

How do you celebrate your successes?

....
....
....
....
....
....
....
....
....
....

What is the most rewarding aspect of overcoming a challenge?

....
....
....
....
....
....
....
....
....
....

Describe a time when you exceeded your own expectations.

....
....
....
....
....
....
....
....
....
....

How do you stay motivated to achieve your goals?

Reflections and Future Hopes

The best is yet to come; the future is full of promise.
– Author Unknown

Place a Picture Here

How do you feel about the journey you've taken in life?

....
....
....
....
....
....
....
....
....
....

What are you most grateful for?

....
....
....
....
....
....
....
....
....
....

How have your priorities changed over time?

....
....
....
....
....
....
....
....
....

What are your hopes for the future?

....
....
....
....
....
....
....
....
....
....

How do you want to be remembered?

....
....
....
....
....
....
....
....
....
....

What are your dreams for your family's future?

....
....
....
....
....
....
....
....
....
....
....

How do you plan to spend your retirement years?

....
....
....
....
....
....
....
....
....

What is on your bucket list?

....
....
....
....
....
....
....
....
....

How do you stay connected with loved ones?

....
....
....
....
....
....
....
....
....
....

How do you stay hopeful and optimistic?

....
....
....
....
....
....
....
....
....
....

What are your thoughts on aging and growing older?

....
....
....
....
....
....
....
....
....
....

How do you maintain a healthy lifestyle?

....
....
....
....
....
....
....
....
....
....

What are your spiritual or philosophical beliefs about life?

....
....
....
....
....
....
....
....
....

How do you find joy and fulfillment in everyday life?

....
....
....
....
....
....
....
....
....
....

What legacy do you hope to leave behind?

Letters to the Ones that I Love

*Family is the compass that guides
us through life's journey.*

– Author Unknown

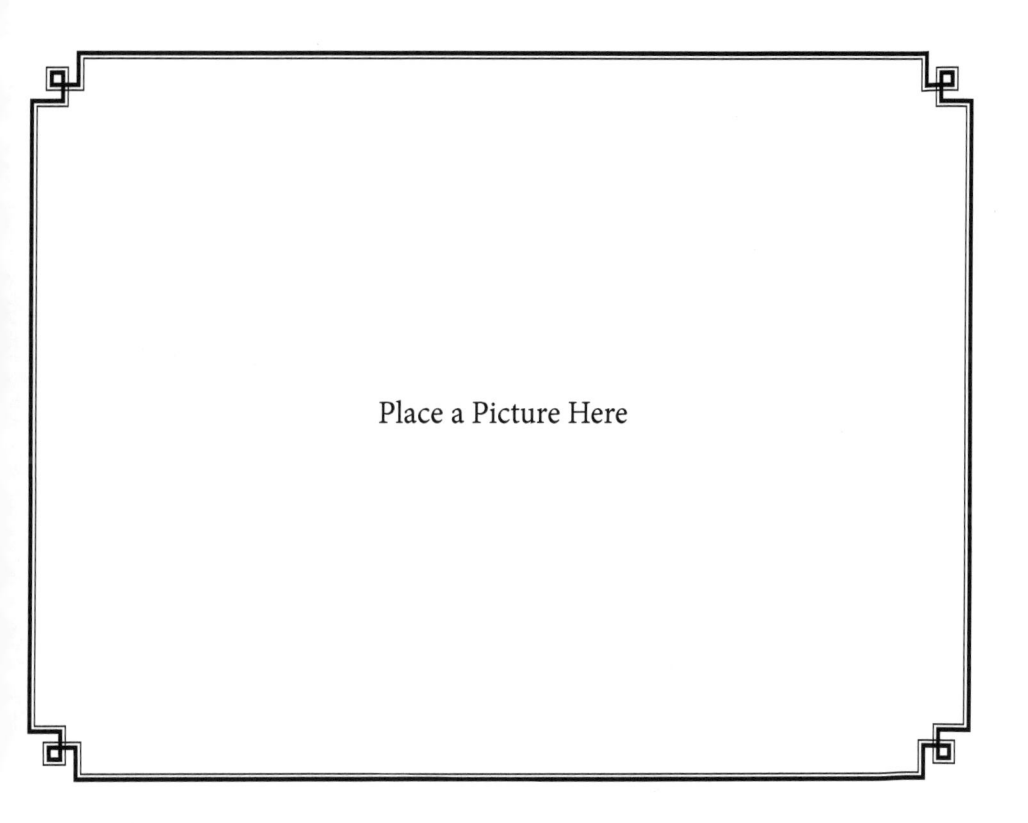

Place a Picture Here

....
....

....
....
....
....
....
....
....
....
....
....
                      ....

A Heartfelt **THANK YOU**

Your decision to purchase and read our book fills us with immense happiness and gratitude. We embarked on this writing endeavor with a vision to inspire, entertain, and touch the lives of our readers. We hope that the world we've created within these pages of our book has captured your imagination and left a lasting impression.

We humbly ask that you take a moment to leave a review on the website where you purchased our book from. Your honest and heartfelt feedback is invaluable to us as authors.

In addition, we invite you to join our community by signing up on our website. Once you've signed up, you will gain exclusive access to a free 50-question trivia challenge. But that's not all. By becoming a member of our community, you will be among the first to receive notifications about new book releases by Abbix Publishing Company.

Thank you for allowing us to be a part of your reading experience. We sincerely hope that our book has brought you joy, awe, and moments of inspiration.

Made in the USA
Columbia, SC
29 June 2024